Extreme GOLF

Dale Concannon

> Golf is the hardest sport.
> One day you're up on cloud
> nine and the next day you
> couldn't scratch a whale's
> belly.
> **Sam Snead**

SUTTON PUBLISHING

Sutton Publishing Limited
Phoenix Mill · Thrupp · Stroud
Gloucestershire · GL5 2BU

First published 2002

Copyright © Dale Concannon

British Library Cataloguing in Publication Data
A catalogue record for this book is available from the British Library

ISBN 0 7509 3159 0

Typeset in 11/14pt Galliard.
Typesetting and origination by
Sutton Publishing Limited.
Printed and bound in England by
J.H. Haynes & Co. Ltd, Sparkford.

For my golfing pal and European Tour professional,
Andrew Beal, a quality individual
on and off the golf course

PHOTOGRAPH CREDITS

All photographs in this book, unless otherwise credited, are from the Phil Sheldon Golf Picture Library or from the Dale Concannon Golf History Archive c/o Phil Sheldon Golf Picture Library, 40 Manor Road, Barnet, EN5 4JQ, United Kingdom, 020 8440 1986.

Please note that while every effort has been made to trace copyright holders, in some rare instances this has not been possible. Therefore we apologise for any omissions that may inadvertently occur.

CONTENTS

A long-lost tradition. Throughout the 1920s and 1930s, top American golfers were based at the Savoy Hotel in London *en route* to British Open, Ryder Cup and Walker Cup matches. As a bit of fun they were often invited to try to drive a ball over the River Thames from the roof – a distance of just under 400 yards. No player ever managed it. The photograph shows American amateur George Von Elm having a go in May 1930.

INTRODUCTION

To the outsider, golf offers none of the heart-thumping excitement of shark fishing off the Florida coast and generates only a fraction of the controversy caused by a disallowed goal at soccer. Yet as anyone who plays it knows, it has a certain something.

Requiring a complete mastery over emotion, nerve and temper, success often depends on the individual's ability to handle all three at once. After all, in what other sport are you expected to drive the ball with the force of a sledgehammer one moment, then execute a chip with the precision of a surgeon's knife the next? Winston Churchill summed it up best when he described golf as 'a game whose aim it is to hit a small ball into an even smaller hole, with weapons ill-designed for the purpose'. As a simple description it cannot be faulted. Each year for countless millions, mastering the sport becomes an absolute obsession. They are destined to spend long hours at the local driving range trying to 'grip it and rip it' like John Daly, and winter evenings are devoted to devouring the latest David Leadbetter teaching manual. Weekends and holidays become family-free zones as all this effort is put into fruitless and ultimately heartbreaking practice.

Describing the extreme effects golf can have, Sir Walter Simpson once observed, 'Nature loses her significance. Rain comes to be regarded solely in terms of putting greens. The daisy is detested, botanical specimens are but hazards. Winds cease to be east, south, west and north. They are ahead, behind or sideways, and the sky is bright or dark according to the state of the game.' How right he was.

On the positive side, golf can be played in splendid isolation from infancy to dotage. Goalposts do not have to be erected and equipment can be kept to a bare minimum. In fact, as long as they have a club and a ball and enough space to enjoy the results, most golfers are perfectly content. Apart from the odd bruised ego, injuries are uncommon and the benefits offered by a strenuous walk are not to be underestimated in this health-conscious age.

In the final analysis, golf is a wonderfully silly game where a little white ball is hit around a field punctuated by yells of quiet desperation. As this book clearly shows, it is an idiosyncratic game where the best and worst of us suffer the same frustrations and the same joys, a game where every shot offers equal potential for glory or disaster. It is simply the best game ever invented.

Dale Concannon

Golf is the hardest game in the world. There's no way you can ever get it. Just when you think you do, the game jumps up and puts you in your place.
Ben Crenshaw

Golf is a funny game. It's done much for health, and at the same time has ruined people by robbing them of their peace of mind. Look at me. I'm the healthiest idiot in the world.
Bob Hope

These are the hazards of golf: The unpredictability of your own body chemistry. The rub of the green on the course. The wind and the weather. The bee that lands on your ball or on the back of your neck while you are putting. The sudden noise while you are swinging. The whole problem of playing the game at high mental tension and low physical tension.
Arnold Palmer

Up close and personal. With the gallery almost within touching distance, Max Faulkner plays his approach to the last hole during the final round of the 1951 British Open at Royal Portrush in Northern Ireland. This was the first and last time golf's oldest major was played outside mainland Britain.

Previous page: Making a splash. American Jim Gallagher has a close encounter of the wet kind at Augusta in 1991.

With a little help from my friends. American Eli Bariteau gets some (illegal) assistance from the gallery on a steep slope at Pebble Beach in the late 1950s.

Golf is a test of temper, a trial of honour, a revealer of character. It affords a chance to play the man and act the gentleman. It means going out into God's out-of-doors, getting close to nature, fresh air, exercise, a sweeping away of the mental cobwebs, genuine recreation of the tired issues. It is a cure for care – an antidote to worry. It includes companionship with friends, social intercourse, opportunities for courtesy, kindliness and generosity to an opponent. It promotes not only physical health but moral force.
David Robertson Forgan

US Open champion in 1937, Ralph Guldahl gets to grips with a difficult lie during practice for the Ryder Cup at Southport and Ainsdale later the same year. Even today, the rules state that you may not stand out of bounds to hit your shot no matter what the obstruction.

The silence of the practice ground. Vijay Singh, one of golf's most dedicated professionals, works long into the evening on the range at Sahalee prior to the final round of the 1988 United States PGA Championship.

Golf is forever throwing up surprise wins but none quite like Jack Fleck's US Open victory in San Francisco in 1955.

A complete unknown, he defeated four-time champion Ben Hogan 69 to 72 in an 18-hole play-off that nobody expected him to win. This is Fleck putting out on the final green; a frustrated Hogan can be seen with his arms crossed on the far right.

What goes up must come down. But don't expect it to come down where you can find it.
Lily Tomlin

Golf is not a mere game; it is a disease, infectious and contagious, which once acquired cannot be shaken off. Once a golfer, always a golfer – there's no help for it.
L. Latchford

I'm over here! Caddie Andy Prodger shows the way at the 1992 Masters at Augusta National. A hundred years before, well-heeled golfers employed a fore-caddie who would stand with a long pole exactly like this and point out where the ball had gone on blind shots.

American Bobby Clampett finds Royal Birkdale really rough going during the later stages of the British Open in 1983.

Young professionals gather nervously around the scoreboard during the 1937 Argentinian Open to see whether they have made the halfway cut. The same ritual is repeated at every tournament today, the only difference being that players now inspect the screen of a laptop computer from the luxury of their hotel suite.

DOWN IN ONE

For most golfers, nothing fires the imagination like a hole-in-one. Whether achieved by sheer luck or great skill, examples of amazing flukes and heart-breaking near misses litter the pages of golf history. One of the most significant came in 1878 when Jamie Anderson was challenging for the lead in the final round of the Open at Prestwick. One shot behind with two holes remaining, he arrived at the penultimate par-3 hole. A young girl in the crowd noticed he had teed up just ahead of the markers. She tugged enthusiastically at her father's jacket and the resulting disturbance caused the young Scot to pull away angrily from his shot. Then, realising she was right and the penalty for such a mistake was disqualification, he re-teed his ball before striking into the cup for an ace. He won by a single stroke from Bob Kirk. The *Ayr Advertiser* later described how Anderson sought out the little girl and thanked her for her help.

Screen legend Gertrude Lawrence was doing some publicity work at the Hollywood Golf Club in the 1930s when somebody suggested that perhaps a golf shot in front of the rolling cameras would be a good idea. Lawrence, who had never picked up a golf club in her life, let alone swung one, innocently agreed. Then, in what must be some sort of record, she holed her first and only golf shot! Unfortunately, the cameraman had only focused on her 'swing' and failed to capture her incredible shot on film. Quite calmly, he asked if she could do it again for the camera!

Golfing legend Harry Vardon always bemoaned his lack of luck when it came to scoring a hole-in-one. (His friend and rival Abe Mitchell had scored 17.) Nearing the end of his career, the six-time Open winner was taken ill with tuberculosis and forced to recuperate at Mundesley Sanatorium in Norfolk. After a few weeks he felt strong enough to play a few holes at a nearby course. Out of practice and still quite weak, Vardon scored his first and last hole-in-one. Those who witnessed it said his reaction was 'more joyous' than when he had won any of his great championships.

With odds against scoring a hole-in-one estimated at around 40,000–1, most golfers might consider an ace beyond them. They could be right. In 1951 a competition was held in New York to settle once and for all the question of whether scoring a hole-in-one is skill or simply dumb luck. Over 1,500 golfers entered a competition with each player – many off low handicaps – given five shots at a selection of par-3 holes. The event was held over three days and included just over 7,000 attempts at scoring a hole-in-one: the nearest ball finished 3 inches away! Proof, if proof were needed, that you cannot fluke a fluke.

One Sunday morning back in the thirties a member of Rochford Golf Club in Essex announced to his pals that he had dreamed of scoring a hole-in-one the night before. Not only that, he knew which hole it was on and even the club he was going to use! It was too good a chance to miss for wagers to be laid and odds were soon given. Then when the fateful hour arrived a large crowd gathered around, curious to see the outcome. Amazingly, the player concerned holed his tee-shot. Was it a fluke? A premonition? Who knows? One thing is for certain – Rochford's par-3 10th was forever afterwards known as the 'Dream Hole'.

Working on the basis that truth is often stranger than fiction, one of the most unusual incidents in hole-in-one history happened before the 1954 United States Open at Baltusrol. Renowned golf architect Robert Trent-Jones had recently added a water hazard to the 185-yard, par-3 4th which involved a long carry from tee to green. Having upset a small but vocal group of members who persistently complained at its severity, he finally volunteered to play the hole himself. A large gallery followed him as he walked on to the back tee, took out an iron club and hit his ball straight into the hole first bounce. 'Gentleman,' said Trent-Jones, 'that should settle all arguments.'

In one of the greatest storms ever seen at the British Open, the heavens poured forth during the Centenary Championship at St Andrews in 1960. Conditions halted play in the final round and the players had to return the following day to finish off the tournament.

Golfing in the rain. Abnormally heavy rain caused the cancellation of the 1950 Trans Mississippi Ladies Championship before the final round. But it failed to dampen the spirits of the competitors. Here tournament leader Patty Berg gets a free ride from her friends.

John Daly attempts the long-distance driving record at Santa Monica Airport prior to the United States PGA Championship at nearby Riviera CC in 1995. Known for his 'grip and rip it' golf swing, 'Wild Thing' was consistently among the longest hitters in the world even when his world ranking slumped in the late 1990s.

The watchful eye of the law keeps everyone in order during the 1994 US Open at Oakmont.

Ready for action. The unmistakable paw of John 'Wild Thing' Daly, photographed on his way to winning the British Open at St Andrews in 1995.

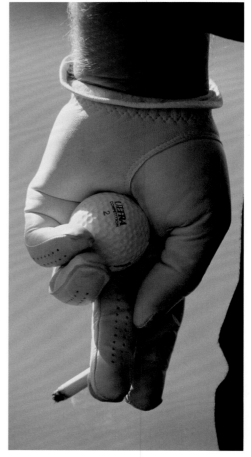

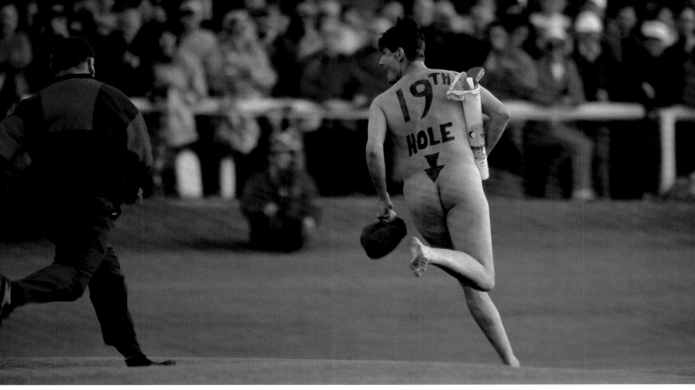

A streaker writes himself into British Open history by providing a new 19th hole at St Andrews in 1995. Worse still, he did it just moments after John Daly had beaten Costantino Rocca in a tense four-hole play-off.

FULL MARKS FOR TRYING

Written large in British Open folklore is happy hacker Maurice Flitcroft. A 46-year-old crane driver from Barrow-in-Furness, he entered the qualifying rounds for the 1976 Championship fully convinced that golf's greatest prize was well within his grasp. The only problem was he had never played a full 18 holes in his life having taken up the game just 16 months earlier. Not surprisingly he took 121 strokes, was immediately disqualified and the £30 entry fee was refunded to his two furious playing partners. With the R&A forced to tighten up procedures, further entries from Flitcroft under the aliases of Gerard Hoppy and Beau Jolley were unearthed over the next few years.

Walter Danecki of Milwaukee gave up his amateur status to compete in the qualifying rounds of the 1965 British Open at Southport and Ainsdale. Some people wish he had not because he took 221 strokes for an 81-over par total. Recording rounds of 108 and 113 he admitted afterwards that he 'felt sad and a little discouraged'. Asked why he had entered he said, 'I wanted the money.'

Artist Harry Rowntree took on the better ball of two former British Open winners off level and won. Receiving an 'allowance' of 150 yards, he trounced Edward Ray and George Duncan at Littlehampton in 1924 by the amazing score of 6&5. Able to pick his ball up at any time, he made a 'hole-in-one' on a par-3 when he 'walked' the ball into the cup after hitting his tee-shot into a greenside bunker! When he was in a ditch he was able to lift and drop for no penalty and when he was out-of-bounds he simply walked it back on to the fairway. For the loss of a few inches he could improve his lie immeasurably. And for the loss of a few more he could hole every putt he ever attempted. Ray commented afterwards that if he had a 'gimme' of 1 yard per round he would win every tournament he ever played in.

◀ Five-time British Open champion James Braid took part in a very unusual challenge match at Sidcup in 1913. It was played in the middle of the night and the only help he received was from the flashlight held by his caddie. He still managed to break 80!

On the eve of the 1931 Ryder Cup match at Scioto, Ohio, some of the best golfers in the world, including Walter Hagen (centre), attend a rather unusual ceremony to celebrate the larger 1.68 golf ball being declared legal in the United States. (It would remain illegal in Britain and the Commonwealth right up to the 1970s where the smaller 1.62 ball reigned supreme.) The picture shows Hollywood film star Marion Shilling teeing-up the new ball for circus performer Jock MacPherson.

A number of top players were invited to tee off over the River Thames to a giant pontoon floating adjacent to Tower Bridge in 1996.

NEVER BET WITH A GOLFER

As if to prove P.T. Barnum's famous saying about there being one sucker born every minute, an unusual bet was offered to the members of Royston Golf Club in 1914. Member John Farrar boasted he could go round the London course in fewer than 100 strokes wearing full army kit issue. An army officer and obviously accustomed to wearing the heavy gear, he offered odds of 10–1 and took a small fortune in bets. Two hours later the round was over and he had won his bet. He then offered a challenge to a local golf professional who failed to break 100 with the result that Farrar took even more money. Perhaps he could have got better odds if he had offered to play in the same outfit as Harry De'ath a few years later. A leading opera singer, he played an inter-club match wearing a full suit of armour.

Renowned Scottish professional Ben Sayers once took a lot of money off an American visitor to Royal Burgess Golf Club in Edinburgh when the man doubted his claim that he could play every hole in four strokes including the par-5s and par-3s. With an interested crowd out following the action, Sayers put together a round of incredible consistency, taking 72 strokes and his doubter's money.

A golf course in the south of England was home to a curious wager when a high handicap golfer bet a professional that he could beat him off level! The only stated condition was that his opponent was required to drink a large whisky and soda on every tee starting at the 1st. Leading by one hole at the time, the pro made it to the 16th tee before finally collapsing in a drunken heap and thus forfeiting the match.

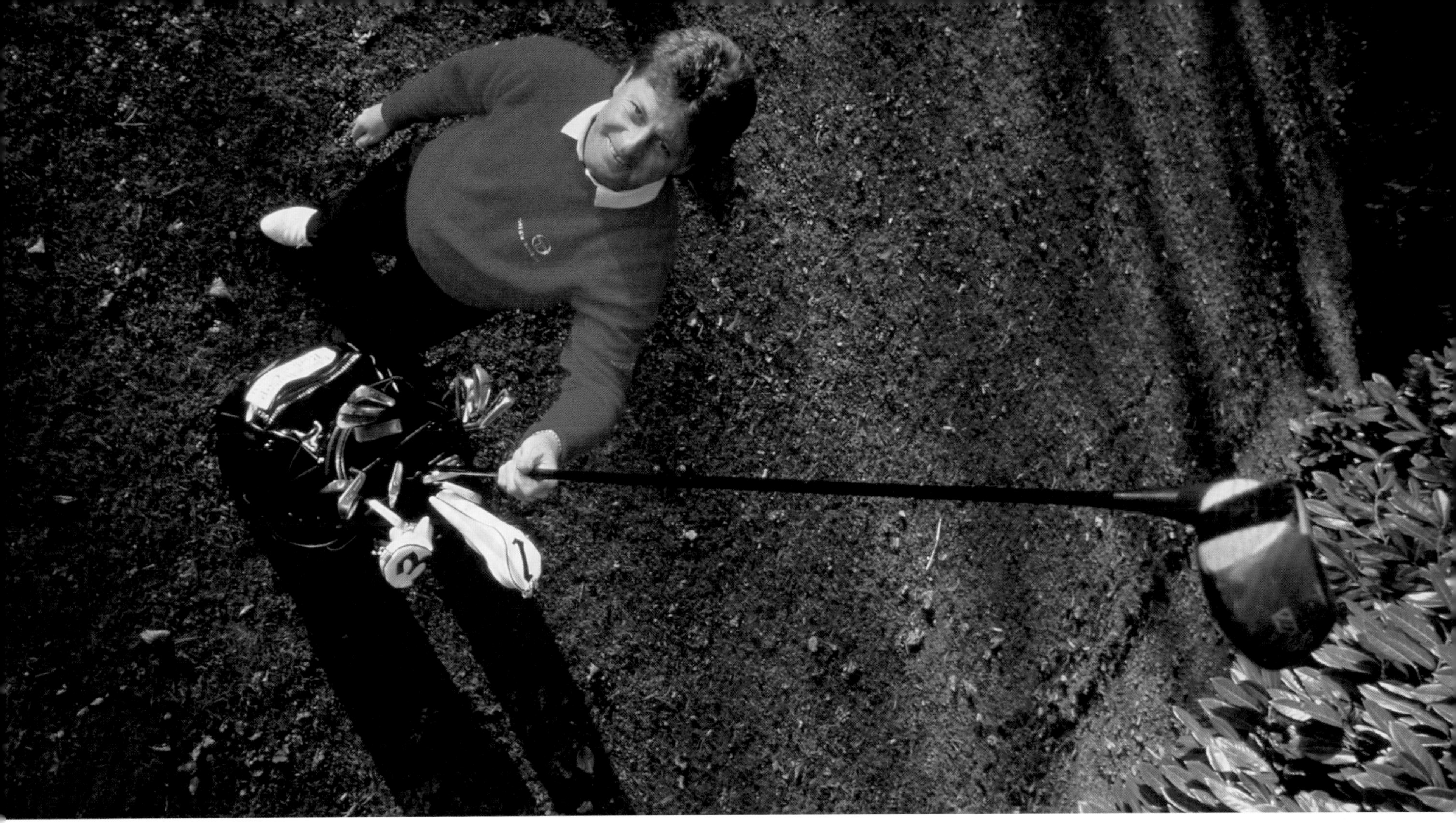

2 Equipped for the Job

Leslie Cotton, brother of three-time British Open Champion Henry, was considered the more talented golfer of the two when they were children. In later life he gave up playing completely to become a well-known coach in South Africa. A passionate trumpet player, he often took the instrument out on the course to help improve the rhythm of those he was coaching. This photograph was taken in the late 1950s.

Previous page: Ian Woosnam shows off a new driver and yes, it really is as long as it looks.

CLUBS

The earliest known set of golf clubs in existence belongs to Royal Troon Golf Club in Scotland. Found wrapped in a newspaper and dating from the early 1700s, they were walled up in a house in Hull back in 1924 and comprise six early 'long-nose' woods and two blacksmith-made irons. Donated to the Scottish club by long-time member Adam Wood, they are thought to be worth in excess of £5 million. On permanent display in the clubhouse for over half a century, they were later moved to the British Golf Museum at St Andrews for security reasons and are now known as 'the ancient clubs'.

Golf has always been an innovative game. As long ago as 1890, inventors looked to make their fortune by designing clubs and balls that would make the game easier to play. With no restrictions on shape, size or the type of materials used, the inventive Victorian mind patented many new ideas including some still in use today, such as metal woods, heel-and-toe weighting and metal shafts. Even hippopotamus-faced irons to glass-headed putters were tried out in an effort to discover the elusive secret of golf.

Shortly after the British Army introduced a new adjustable aiming sight for its Enfield rifle in 1890, a Scottish company called Urquhart used the same technology to develop a revolutionary 'all-in-one' golf club. At a time when golfers thought nothing of carrying twenty or more clubs in their bag, the iron-headed innovation could be altered to play anything from pitch-shots to putts. It was a wonderful idea in theory, but the company finally went bust because the mechanism used to alter the club's loft had a tendency to seize up in the rain!

Probably the hardest hard-luck story in golf history involved a 38-year-old blacksmith from Edinburgh called Thomas Horsburgh. A renowned golfer he invented the first steel-shafted golf clubs as early as 1894. They were little more than solid steel rods, but he also developed a method by which they could be retracted from the wooden club head at will and used in another club. However, the young blacksmith failed to persuade any local professionals to commend his invention. We shall never know whether the professionals' reluctance was born of apathy, or a fear that the new shafts would threaten their already meagre livelihood fitting wooden ones to clients' clubs. However, it is certain that after spending all his money developing the idea, Horsburgh ended up in a debtors' prison. Fortunately, his later invention – the nail-less horseshoe – restored his finances and he died leaving the substantial sum of £14,000 in his will.

Swimmers wear Teflon swimsuits these days. Badminton rackets are made of boron. If you want to excel in sport, it seems you need to embrace modern technology. Not so on the golf course. A recent survey revealed that almost a third of the players on the PGA Tour in America used putters in excess of 20 years old, more in some cases! So with all the space-age materials available why do top pros prefer these relics of a bygone era? Perhaps it's the extra 'feel' they offer, or the better quality strike of the putter face. Then again, it could be that players have heard what a fantastic investment clubs can offer. Today, the most collectible putters are models used by a famous player at his peak: Jack Nicklaus, for example, used a George Low Sportsman Wizard 600 for many of his major wins. A simple-looking blade putter with a silver-coloured head and the company name picked out in black paint, it could be bought new for about $50. These putters are currently valued at between £4,000 and £5,000 each!

◄ Golf ringers. Offered as a novel method to improve accuracy, two teaching professionals at White Sulphur Springs take turns to chip balls through a fire alarm hoop in the 1920s.

▶ Okay, I'm ready for you now. David Leadbetter and his instruments of torture pictured at his teaching base at Lake Nona, Florida, in 1992. One of the best-known teachers around, it was David's success with Nick Faldo in the early 1990s that helped cement his reputation.

Never known for his ability on the greens, the legendary Arnold Palmer shows off a small part of his putter collection.

REUNITED AT LAST

Merion, 1950. Ben Hogan was playing in his first United States Open Championship since a terrible car accident almost robbed him of his life 16 months earlier. In what proved a highly emotional comeback, the American needed a par-4 on the demanding final hole to join Lloyd Mangrum and George Fazio in a play-off. With huge crowds threatening to swamp the fairway, he followed up a solid drive with a superb one-iron approach to the green. Hogan then two-putted before winning the play-off the following day with a 69. The club he used to play his winning approach shot – later nominated as the 'shot of the century' – was stolen shortly after. Despite Hogan's many appeals for its return, and the offer of a large reward, the famous club remained lost for well over three decades. It finally turned up in 1983 when a pro from Indiana found it among a bunch of rusty second-hand items bought for his shop. It was stamped 'Hogan' on the back and the finder was intrigued by the golf-ball-size indent worn out on the club's sweet-spot: someone had obviously practised with it for many long hours. He contacted the Hogan Company in Texas and the player soon confirmed that it was indeed his club. Later donated to the USGA Golf Museum in New Jersey, it remains on permanent display.

If you watch a game, it's fun. If you play it, it's recreation. If you work at it, it's golf.
Bob Hope

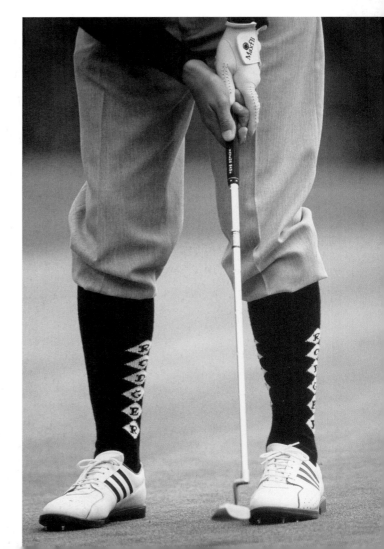

Known for his sartorial style (or lack of it?) Australian Rodger Davis often played wearing plus-four trousers and long woollen socks. At the Spanish Open in 1990 at the Club de Campo, Malaga, he even had his name on his socks in case anyone forgot who he was.

➠ An ingenious golf fan finds a way of watching the golf at the 1988 US Open at Brookline, Massachusetts.

◖ A common site at every major sporting event all over the world, professional photographers get in position at the 1994 British Open at Turnberry.

➠ A load of balls. The Ryder Cup is one of the best-organised events on the golfing calendar and everything has its place as this practice ground shot taken at Valderrama in 1997 shows.

Golf is 20 per cent mechanics and technique. The other 80 per cent is philosophy, humour, tragedy, romance, melodrama, companionship, camaraderie, cussedness, and conversation.
Grantland Rice

◖ The only way to travel. Obviously on child-minding duty, this Scottish golf fan finds a clever way of following the action at the 1987 British Open at Muirfield.

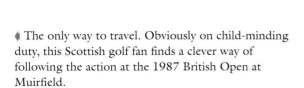

BALLS

Cleveland sportsman Coburn Haskell, the driving force behind a revolutionary new golf ball, first patented his invention in 1899. Designed with a central rubber core around which bands of elastic were stretched, it was the forerunner of the ball in use today. Hoping to make his fortune, Haskell spent at least three months a year for the next decade defending his patent in courts in both Britain and America.

As with any new idea, feathery ball makers proved reluctant to embrace the new gutta-percha in the mid-1800s. Well-known professional Allan Robertson even paid young caddies a few pennies to bring in lost gutties so he could burn them at night in his workshop.

Long before golf's rule-makers began regulating equipment, maverick ball designers came up with all sorts of innovative ideas for the cover, including star patterns, half-moons, diamonds, concentric circles and even aeroplane propellers. One was even moulded in the shape of the Earth, continents and all, including the North and South Poles.

'Old' Tom Morris is one of the game's legendary figures. Born in 1821 he probably saw and created more golf history in his eight decades than any other player connected with the Royal and Ancient game. He was in turn an apprentice feathery ball maker, a caddie, a legendary tournament player, a golf course designer and, if that were not enough, father to the greatest golfer of his generation, 'Young' Tom Morris.

OLD EQUIPMENT AT NEW PRICES

Today, golf antiques are big business with an estimated £25 million spent every year at auction, via the Internet or through private sale. In July 1984 Sotheby's, London, sold 'An unusual hexagonal-faced gutta-percha golf ball' for £280. Twelve years later at Phillips, New York, the same ball (a Willie Park 'Royal') sold for a massive £21,784 – a huge percentage return on the investment in anyone's language.

In 1992 Sotheby's held a golfing memorabilia valuation event at its offices in Edinburgh. Halfway through the day a local man popped in with a handful of wooden-shafted clubs in a tatty canvas bag. Imagine his surprise when one of them turned out to be an extremely rare blacksmith-made iron from the early 1700s. Valued at around £30,000 it eventually sold to Jamie Ortiz-Patino, billionaire owner of Valderrama Golf Club in Spain, for £84,000. The original owner commented afterwards how he had kept the club in his garden shed for years and it was only brought out when his grandchildren wanted something to dig up the garden with!

NEVER MAKE A PROMISE YOU DON'T WANT TO KEEP

During the 1973 Ryder Cup at Muirfield a confident Lee Trevino boasted he would 'kiss the American team's asses' if he didn't beat Peter Oosterhuis in their singles match the following day. The record book shows that he halved the match and his team members – including Jack Nicklaus and Arnold Palmer – jokingly said that he should keep his promise.

A grandstand performance. At major golf events like the British Open or Ryder Cup, hosts of young people are employed to pick up all the rubbish that accumulates throughout the tournament. Rarely does an old crisp packet or plastic bottle hit the ground without one of them on hand to spirit it away, as this young man shows during the 1995 British Open at St Andrews.

American professional Tommy Bolt used to say that hitting the ball into water was like a 'real car smash' compared with the mere 'fender-bender' of hitting it into the trees. At least it provides a good living for this professional ball diver in Sun City, South Africa.

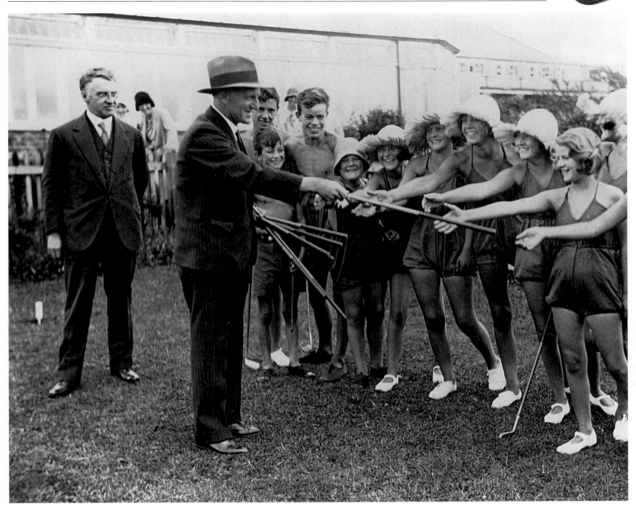

Spreading the gospel. A local professional hands out putters for a junior-golf tournament at a holiday camp in Skegness in 1932.

Golf from its own peculiar character of sport requires a large variety of implements called clubs to move, by devious and dextrous hits, a very small ball through an adventurous journey, over undulating ground, from a starting place called the 'tee' into a hole of irritatingly small dimensions cut in the turf.
Robert Harris

Yes, it is a cruel game, one in which the primitive instincts of man are given full play, and the difference between golf and fisticuffs is that in one the pain is of the mind and in the other it is of the body.
Henry Leach

♦ The golfing pram. In 1920 a newspaper advert described the benefits of this novel invention for women golfers: 'Considering how difficult it would be for "mum" to get away for a game of golf, the Dunkley Golfing Pram allows baby to come along for the ride. Comfortable and easy to carry, you need never miss a round on the links ever again.' Quite where 'mum' put her golf clubs is another question entirely.

◆ Carrying a golf bag larger than himself, this little boy was from a well-to-do family (as his clothing shows). The picture was taken around 1910; very few of the poorly paid urchins who trudged barefoot around British golf courses at this time would have been in the mood to raise a smile.

◆ President Eisenhower's passion for golf was well known and golfing gifts like this oversize bag occasionally turned up at the White House. This was a gift from Argentina in 1956, and the hapless official given the job of accepting it looks a little overwhelmed.

◆ It's in the bag: Mark Roe was told to use less leg-action on his downswing and took the advice a bit too literally at the 1987 Benson & Hedges International at Fulford.

A friendly round at the disused Kabul Golf Club after the liberation of Afghanistan in 2001. The game was staged by war correspondents and the old man hitting a chip was the caddie master at the nine-hole course before the Taleban regime declared golf un-Islamic.

Some golfers admit they would fly to the moon and back just to get a game. In 1971 astronaut Alan B. Shepard did just that. An avid golfer, he managed to smuggle a makeshift club and a couple of balls aboard Apollo 14. Concerned the extra weight would show up on Mission Control monitors, he created the club from items already in the module, with the exception of a genuine six-iron head. The grip was a tool used to scoop up soil samples, while the shaft was assembled from five separate pieces of aluminium tubing. The two Dunlop 65 golf balls were smuggled into the capsule in a toolbox. Near the end of the second moonwalk, and just before entering the module for the last time, he hit two balls with fellow astronaut Edgar Mitchell looking on in amazement. The first was a complete miss-hit that landed in a nearby crater. The second was hit squarely, and in the one-sixth gravity of the moon it flew 'miles and miles'. The club now occupies pride of place in the USGA Museum at Far Hills, New Jersey with the actual brand of the head still a closely guarded secret because NASA did not want any commercial gain made from the incident.

I think I'll put some backspin on this chip. Two of the greatest showmen in the history of golf, Walter Hagen (left) and Joe Kirkwood (far right) clown around with the oversize clubs they used in their exhibition matches.

VISION OF THE FUTURE

In 1892 an amazing little book entitled *Golf in the Year 2000* was penned by British author John McCullough. Describing the adventures of fanatical golfer, Alexander Gibson, it tells how he fell into a coma only to wake up over 100 years later. Understandably, the world had changed beyond recognition except for two things – golf was still a popular pastime and St Andrews was still its spiritual home. Outlining an incredible vision of the future, the book predicts, among other things, metal-headed woods and even live televised golf from America! All this in the bygone days of wooden-shafted clubs, crude leather golf bags and gutta-percha balls! In one chapter McCullough details the forerunner to the modern electric golf trolley:

'It was a funny sight to see four men stalking along followed by what looked like toy tricycles. . . . On this contrivance the clubs were carried . . . they simply followed wherever we went . . . and regulated themselves to our pace, stopped when we stopped and so on. My friend explained that we had a sort of magnet behind our jackets which attracted them but at the same time did not allow them to come closer than 12-feet.'

Substitute a remote control and you could be playing golf in modern-day Florida.

Like his great rival Harry Vardon, J.H. Taylor (far right) believed in spreading the gospel of golf far and wide. Here he can be seen competing in Egypt on sand greens in 1905.

It is a thousand pities that neither Aristotle nor Shakespeare was a golfer. There is no game that strips the soul so naked.
Horace Hutchinson

A barefoot caddie from Ceylon in the 1920s. Dressed in a hand-me-down woman's jacket, one of his main jobs would have been to find lost balls in the cobra-infested rough.

Previous page: Up a gum tree without a golf club. Bernhard Langer refused to declare his ball unplayable during the 1981 Benson & Hedges tournament at Fulford near York. Moments later the German had chipped his ball out from between the branches and only narrowly failed to save his par.

UNUSUAL HAZARDS

Scottish professional Jimmy Stewart was competing in the 1972 Singapore Open when his ball caught the attention of a cobra that mistook it for an egg. Bravely dispatching the large snake with one blow of his club he was amazed to see another, smaller snake wriggle out from its mouth. Repeating the exercise, Stewart went on to finish his round.

Early in the second round of the 1949 British Open at Royal St George's Harry Bradshaw sliced his drive on the 5th and unluckily found his ball inside the bottom half a broken beer bottle. Pondering the lie for less than a minute he decided to smash it out rather than refer to the rulebook – which would have given him a free drop under the outside agency ruling. He was only able to advance the ball a few yards down the fairway and the resultant double-bogey cost him outright victory the following day after he lost in a play-off to South African star Bobby Locke. Sadly, the Irishman never came close to winning again.

Noted Scottish amateur Freddie Tait, whose brilliant career was cut short during the Boer War, once found his ball lodged in the bottom of condensed milk can after a wayward approach shot. He decided to chip it forward and the can landed on the green. Seconds later the ball popped out and ran obligingly close to the cup.

An uphill struggle. While golf courses are much longer today than a century ago, bunkers then were far more punitive than manicured modern sand traps. And golfers were not allowed to smooth over footprints and other marks, even in major tournaments like the British Open. This photograph from the 1880s was a posed effort for a magazine, but you get the idea.

Left: Don't hit it left whatever you do: Fred Couples successfully avoids the water that borders the spectacular 18th at Sawgrass during the 1984 Tournament Players' Championship. *Right:* Some hazards are worse than others. This poisonous snake was captured during the US Open at Congressional in 1997.

☚ Normally a player enters the recorder's tent after the round to hand in his scorecard but Mark James had other ideas at the 1992 Volvo Masters at Valderrama. Playing the final hole he overshot the green and rather than have the whole structure decamped, he bravely chose to play his ball. He got up and down for par.

◀ The aptly named Dorothy Oaks found herself up a tree in San Francisco in 1925 but appears to have been determined to play the ball where it lay.

With instructional golf videos still six decades away, Henry Cotton shows how to 'explode' a shot from the bunker for the Movietone Corporation in 1932. Note the microphone on the left to catch his comments.

No slave ever scanned the expression of a tyrannical master with half the miserable anxiety with which the golfer surveys the ground over which the hole is to be approached. He looks at the hole from the ball, and he looks at the ball from the hole. No blade of grass, no scarcely perceptible inclination of the surface, escapes his critical inspection.
Arthur Balfour

The fabulous Emirates Golf Club in Dubai. Built in the middle of the desert it needs millions of gallons of water each month just to survive. Now home to one of the world's most prestigious events – The Dubai Desert Classic – top names like Tiger Woods, Ernie Els and Colin Montgomerie have all sung its praises.

What snow? Hardy south coast golfers don't let a little snow and ice put them off their game at Rye in 1988.

Can't see the wood for the trees. A suitably well-dressed Miss Cradock-Hartopp plays her way out of trouble during the London Ladies' Foursomes at Wentworth in 1935.

Where did you say the hole was, caddie? One golfer took the scenic route when playing at Pebble Beach in the 1930s.

I know the fairway is here somewhere. Legendary golf course architect
Harry Shapland Colt (centre) supervises work on the 15th fairway on
the West Course at Wentworth. Constructing the 15th was an
incredibly laborious job and explosives were used to clear stubborn
tree-stumps from what is now the fairway. Perhaps this is why the
course has long been known as 'The Burma Road'.

TAKE THE SHOT AND FACE THE CONSEQUENCES

Mathieu Boya hit possibly the most expensive shot in history. As a youth he practised next to the Benin Air Base. In 1987 he struck a bird in flight with a particularly fierce drive and the unfortunate animal landed in the open cockpit of a Mirage jet fighter attempting to take off. The startled pilot lost control, smashed into four jet fighters parked on the ground and completely wiped out the entire Benin Air Force in one blow at an estimated cost of $200 million. Boya was later jailed and told that he would only be released when he agreed to pay all the damages.

During a tournament, top Scottish amateur Freddie Tait drove a ball through a man's hat and was forced to give the owner five shillings to buy a new one. Grumbling about the cost, he was reminded by his friend Old Tom Morris that 'the price of an oak coffin' would have been far more.

Known for his repertoire of amazing trick-shots, professional George Ashdown played a full round at Esher in 1931 striking each shot off the forehead of his trusting assistant, Ena Shaw. She lay flat on the ground with a rubber tee strapped to her head.

THE 'WRONG' WAY ROUND

Considered the 'Home of Golf', the Old Course at St Andrews has one unique feature – it can be played either way round. It was common practice to play even major competitions over the so-called 'left-handed' course, starting at the 18th. Indeed the British Amateur Championship, won by Horace Hutchinson, was mistakenly played on it in 1988 when, according to the rota, the 'normal' right-handed one should have been used. Even today, the Royal and Ancient sets aside a week or two each summer for club members to play the 'wrong' way round.

LANDED HERE

A true action shot. Spectators found themselves under fire at Wentworth when Ryder Cup veteran Sam King bounced his drive off someone's head during a professional tournament just after the war. What makes the picture remarkable are the animated poses of the people in the gallery as they struggle to get out of the way.

A tolerable day, a tolerable green, a tolerable opponent, supply, or ought to supply, all that any reasonably constituted human being should require in the way of entertainment. With a fine sea view, and a clear course in front of him, the golfer should find no difficulty in dismissing all worries from his mind.
Arthur Balfour

Overleaf: The poor cousin of the spectacular Emirates Club, Dubai Country Club boasts sand greens and sand tees and a warning to watch out for camels crossing the fairway.

➤ 'Divotees' of golf at Upminster are warned in no uncertain terms to obey the rules in 1938.

◀ Can someone tell me where the hole is please? The flamboyant Babe Zaharias shows a novel way to putt during an exhibition match in Atlanta, Georgia in 1959.

➤ Legendary Scottish comedian Neil Kenyon gets to grips with a tricky lie at Wembley Golf Links in 1912. The course was ploughed under in 1920 to make way for the new Empire Stadium which opened three years later.

In the United States in the late 1920s golf became a game for the successful company executive but often he could not get away from his desk to play a full round. In 1928 his prayers were answered when two American entrepreneurs named Drake Delanoy and John Ledbetter developed this cottonseed-turf putting course on top of a New York skyscraper. The idea proved a huge hit and was copied in cities all over America.

A tricky putt. Larry Semon poses for a publicity still for his latest film *Golf* (1922), which also starred Oliver Hardy. Semon was a hugely popular star in the silent movie era and this was just one of many flicks which used golf as a vehicle for humour.

Long before he became King George VI, the Duke of York was asked to hit the opening drive at a new public golf course in Richmond Park in 1923. In line with tradition, the caddie who secured the ball was rewarded with a golden sovereign and by the look of his ragged trousers he needed it. The photograph shows a smiling duke handing over the coin with five-time British Open champion J.H. Taylor looking on (far left).

Long before Tiger-mania there was Bobby Jones. A lifelong amateur he was the most popular golfer in the world by the time he won his legendary Grand Slam in 1930. Followed by adoring crowds wherever he played, here he is being helped off the course by two constables after beating Roger Wethered in the final of the British Amateur in St Andrews that wonderful year.

Previous page:
Extreme golf personified. Tiger Woods celebrates in typically exuberant style after holing the winning putt in the 1998 Johnnie Walker Classic at the Blue Canyon Course in Phuket, Thailand. He beat South African Ernie Els in a tense play-off and his fist-pumping reaction symbolises his incredible drive and desire to win.

AGAINST THE ODDS

No golfer, man or woman, ever came closer to attaining mythical status than Babe Zaharias. In a life cut tragically short by cancer at just forty-five, she out-ran, out-jumped and, for a time, out-golfed a whole generation. Following gold medal success at hurdles and javelin in the 1932 Olympic Games, she was persuaded to take part in an exhibition golf match in Florida a short time later. Matched against Walter Hagen and her legendary namesake, baseball star Babe Ruth, she consistently out-drove both men. She was a relative novice in golfing terms and a sport reporter asked her how she generated such huge distances off the tee. 'All I know,' she said, pointing at her chest, 'if it wasn't for these, I'd hit it 30 yards further!'

In one of the great golfing comebacks of all time, professional Andrew Beal lost an eye to cancer in December 2001, then returned to score a hole-in-one at the Great North Open at Slaley Hall in June the following year. He then became the only one-eyed golfer to make the halfway cut in a PGA European Tour event.

Two birdies in a row? During the qualifying round for the One Armed Golfers' Championship in 1935 J.W. Perret killed a seagull with his approach shot to the first green. Ten minutes later he did exactly the same on the second hole.

ANALYSIS AND PRACTICE

Happy hacker Robert Russell took up golf in his mid-forties and went on to become one of the best-selling authors on the sport. Studying the methods of top players he found that every one, no matter how he or she swung the club, had excellent posture and balance at address. Applying his findings to his own meagre game he quickly reduced his handicap to scratch before *Golf Monthly* asked him to explain his ideas in a regular feature. Written under the pen-name of 'Mr X', his column proved an instant hit and ran for years. Russell followed up with three books on the subject, all of which became best-sellers in Britain and the United States. He continued to 'shoot his age' even in his mid-70s.

Try this for your nerves. Sam Snead shows off his party trick of balancing one ball on top of another during the Los Angeles Open in 1937. The test was used as a tension-breaker by the legendary American golfer; his record was six balls piled up this way!

Overleaf: Into the bear pit. American players, caddies and fans go crazy after Justin Leonard holes the match-winning putt against Jose Maria Olazábal in the 1999 Ryder Cup at Brookline, Massachusetts. This was a hugely controversial encounter between Europe and the United States, and complaints about the Americans running across the 17th green in this way echoed through the normally sedate world of golf for many months to come. With the atmosphere likened to 'a Bear Pit', the damage done to the image of golf has been immeasurable.

That certain style. Two women golfers competing in the 1934 LGU County Championship Finals at Skegness show an intensity that any top professional would be proud of – especially the one standing a little too close to the action.

IT GETS INTO THE BLOOD

Golfing pals William Chamberlain and George New played a nine-hole match at Littlecote Golf Club every Thursday for sixteen years from 1922 to 1938. Recording every stroke, they played 814 rounds with Chamberlain taking the honours 44,008 shots to his rival's 42,371.

Chicago judge Joseph Sabath ruled in 1925 that, 'golf widowhood is not yet grounds for divorce' even though the 'husband is a hopeless duffer with a wretched drive, who spends most of his time on the golf course'.

Now what do I do? Professional Alex Herd ponders his next shot during a tournament at Mitcham, South London in 1920.

Sorry, I left my purse at home. A disgruntled caddie looks as though he is not going to get paid at Royal Wimbledon in 1930.

Costantino Rocca holes a monster putt off the 72nd green at St Andrews during the 1995 British Open to tie the lead. A former factory worker from Bergamo, Italy, he eventually lost to John Daly in a four-hole play-off for the title and his chance of major glory.

♦ Jean Van de Velde on his way to losing a two-shot lead in the final round at the 1999 British Open at Carnoustie. Able to double-bogey the par-4 18th hole and win, Van de Velde visited the rough, the grandstand, the burn and a greenside bunker in that order before carding a triple-bogey 7. This took him into a three-man play-off which he lost to the eventual champion Paul Lawrie who started the last day ten shots behind the tournament lead. Some weeks later the Frenchman was invited to play the hole using just a putter and made a 6!

BEWARE OF A WAGER

Golf and gambling have often gone hand in hand. The urge to bet that you can play a hole in fewer strokes than your partner has proved irresistible to all of us at one time or another. However, what stake are you prepared to lay down? The records of the Royal and Ancient Golf Club of St Andrews tell of one wager in 1870 in which Sir David Moncreiffe bet his life against that of John Whyte-Melville. The eventual winner was to present a new silver golf club to the members. The record books omit to tell us who actually won the match but thirteen years after it was played John Whyte-Melville gave a speech in which he expressed his deep regret at the death of Sir David Moncreiffe and, perhaps more significantly, 'the causes that led to it'.

In 1766 the Honourable Company of Edinburgh Golfers went as far as to ban the amount one golfer could win off another in a day's play. It seems that far too many duels were being fought between members to settle their disputes. Unfortunately, this ruling did not allow for the ingenuity of golfing gamblers who soon found a way round it. With the limit set on how much you could win in 'one-day's play', matches were played over three holes at night with the caddies holding a lantern to show the way! The Society of St Andrews Golfers realised that no one would play golf if it tried to ban on-course gambling, but finally lost patience in 1822 when one member used the club's committee book to record the terms of his bet!

Challenge matches between professionals became increasingly popular in the second half of the nineteenth century with huge sums riding on the outcome of individual or four-ball games. Well supported at each venue, the most popular matches were those between Old Tom Morris and his great rival Willie Park. With vast sums bet on the outcome the large galleries were not averse to a little skulduggery to influence the final result. At Musselburgh in 1855, for example, a match turned into a riot after Park's supporters started kicking his opponent's ball into the rough when the match was going against the home player. The St Andrews man refused to play on and retired to a nearby pub while the police tried to achieve some order. Park then told Morris that unless he continued with the match he would have to forfeit the £500 prize money! Morris refused to be persuaded and Park played on alone. Grabbing the money as he holed out on the final green, Park was extremely fortunate to escape with his life.

In 1907 the great English amateur John Ball Jnr boasted he could go round his home course, Royal Liverpool, in under 90 strokes, inside three hours and without losing a ball. At the time the course was blanketed in a thick sea fog. In spite of the circumstances the player went ahead with the wager and a large crowd looked on as he teed-up a ball he had painted black especially for such an occasion. Halfway around the sun broke through and cleared the mist. Ball took full advantage, went round in 81 in just over two hours and won his bet. Royal Liverpool was also the venue for another strange wager a few years later. In a match played off level between a scratch player and a six-handicapper the latter had the right to shout 'boo!' three times during the game. With a small fortune riding on the result the six-handicap golfer saved up his 'advantage' until the 13th hole where he used up his first 'boo!'. The scratch player was so on edge because he was waiting for the next two shouts that he lost his nerve and the match.

In September 1874 Jack Bloxham of Royal Aberdeen Golf Club backed himself to play 12 rounds of golf inside 24 hours topped off by a 10-mile walk. He completed the task with three hours to spare.

◖ A woman's work is never done. This is a publicity still from the 1920s movie short *Love in the Rough*.

David Feherty takes a break at the Benson & Hedges International Open at St Mellion in 1993. A former Ryder Cup golfer, the Irishman's easy-going style has proved a huge hit with American fans in his new role as television pundit.

FORGOT HOW TO PLAY

Tour professional George Burns found himself thinking the unthinkable before the final round of the Tournament Players' Championship in 1979. Arriving at the first tee, the burly American, who was only three shots behind the leader Lanny Wadkins, had forgotten how to play golf! It was absurd and he knew it but no matter how much he tried, he could not get comfortable enough over the ball to make a swing. With his playing partners waiting patiently on the tee, the situation was becoming desperate. Eventually he managed to move the ball forward and somehow scrambled around in 83. Describing it as 'the worst day of my life', Burns even considered walking off halfway through the round but decided against it. It is not clear what happened to him that day but the following week he scored 67 in the opening round at the Heritage Classic and the crisis was over.

Long known as an ice-cold competitor, Nick Faldo reveals the drama and emotion involved in holing a winning putt in the 1989 World Match Play Championship at Wentworth.

A matter of honour. Silent movie actor Ernie Adams is shown blowing hard on the ball to try to keep it out of the hole. Unfortunately, he is losing the match at this point and has to win if he is to marry one of the young ladies present – definitely against the rules. Perhaps someone should have told the object of desire what damage high heels do to a putting green! Golf was a popular subject for film makers back in the early 1920s.

Baseball reveals character; golf exposes it.
Ernie Banks

Who says flower power is dead? Lennie Clements and his laid-back caddie at the 1988 Tournament Players'
Championship at Sawgrass.

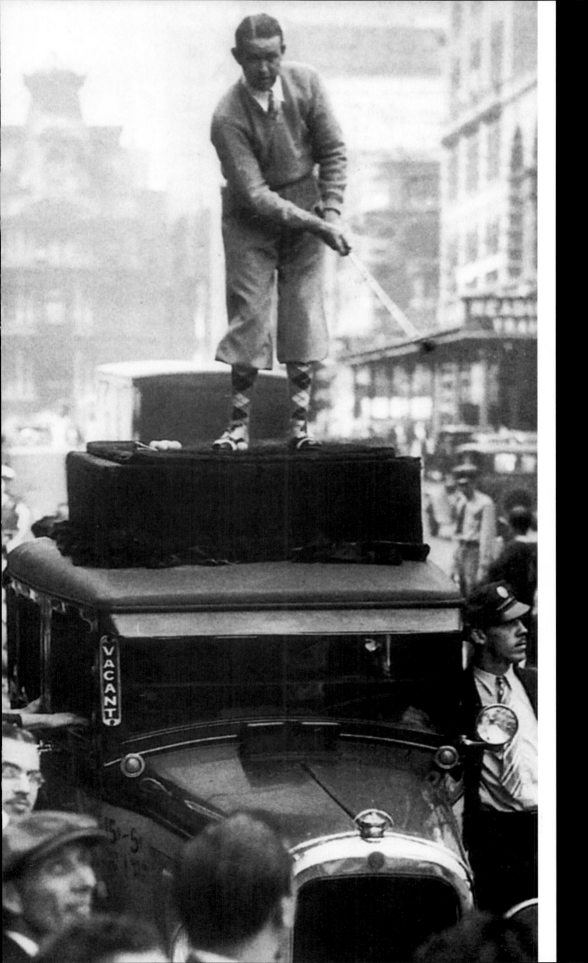

From 1900 onwards the popularity of golf spread like wildfire to countries around the globe, including Argentina. In a scene repeated in India, Ceylon, Scotland and the United States, this photograph from 1928 shows a group of caddy boys ready for action.

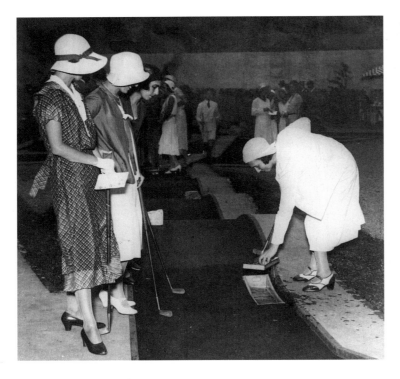

As golf's popularity increased in the early twentieth century, a new phenomenon emerged in the form of mini-golf. (Indoor golf would follow later.) In the 1920s these glorified putting greens sprang up all over the United States with competitions held for men, women and juniors. It was considered hugely fashionable and stylish women thought nothing of playing putt-putt in high heels and a fur wrap.

⬧ When Bobby Jones won his legendary Grand Slam of British and American Open and Amateur Championships in 1930 it was thought a new golden age of golf had been born. To celebrate this new beginning, *Golfing* magazine in Britain carried this wonderfully evocative image on its front cover showing the old year looking on as the sprightly youngster clips away a well-struck iron shot. Sadly, *Golfing*'s enthusiasm was misplaced. Jones took the decision to retire at twenty-eight and the decade ended in war.

Previous page: Riding high. Trick-shot artist Alex Morrison drumming up business for his one-man show in New York in the 1920s.

Start 'em young. Four Scottish youngsters get a taste of the Royal and Ancient game at Dunbar in 1915.

HOT SHOTS

In 1928 a group of American enthusiasts dropped golf balls from an aeroplane on to Westbury Golf Club in New York course, betting on who could finish closest to each hole. They wrapped the balls in cloth so they did not bounce and the match was eventually won three-up by the team captained by William Hammond. Three years later Captain Pennington of the Royal Air Force took part in a similar match at Sonning near Reading. Competing against club professional Arthur Young who was down on the ground, he took 80 balls up in his plane and dropped them on to the green via his bomb hatch. Exactly how this worked is not clear but the record books show that he went round in 29 strokes compared to his rival's highly creditable 68.

A one-legged golfer finds his disability no bar to playing good golf at Rye in 1950.

Sheikh Abdallah was an avid golfer who reputedly took his seven sons out to play every morning. Here he is hitting balls at the Helwan Golf Club, Egypt, in 1939. Today they would call it aversion therapy.

DID I TELL YOU ABOUT THE TIME . . . ?

In 1920 the Golf Tee Company of New York produced a brochure entitled 'Listening Rates for Golf'. The brochure was published purely as a joke to promote the company's tees and pencils, but the firm was inundated with calls from desperate golfers looking for a sympathetic ear. Executives placed a time limit of 5 minutes for a description of a single shot and 15 minutes for an entire round. Here is a sample of the services offered and prices charged:

LISTENING TO:

Long drives	25 cents
Beautiful approaches	50 cents
Long putts sunk	35 cents
Short putts missed	50 cents
Getting out of rough	15 cents
Getting out of a bunker	45 cents
Almost a 'hole-in-one'	$2.00

QUALIFIED RATES (Describing 18 holes, hole by hole)

Under 90	$1.00
Between 91 and 100	$1.50
Over 100	$2.00
Description of Vacation Golf	$2.50

SPECIAL RATES – For Hard Luck Golf Stories detailing: describing bad lies; unethical opponents; out-of-bounds; landing in the rough; looking up; disturbance on tee-shot.

Just listening	15 cents each
Listening with sincerity	35 cents each
Listening to description of shots by opponents that were (in your opinion) lucky	10 cents per shot
Listening to description of shots by opponents that were *actually* lucky	three for 10 cents.

LISTENING TO:

What's wrong with the course	50 cents
What's wrong with the clubhouse	$1.00
What's wrong with my playing partners	$1.00

PARTICULARLY DIFFICULT LISTENING ITEMS PLEASE APPLY FOR HOURLY RATES:

For example, listening to phrases like 'if the caddy held the pin' or 'if I didn't top the ball' or 'if the ball didn't rim the cup' or 'if I hadn't sliced the ball etc.'.

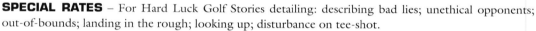

The trouble with me is I think too much.
I always said you have to be dumb to play good golf.
JoAnne Carner

In the 1950s office workers were encouraged to get out at lunchtime and enjoy some fresh air in smog-ridden London. To make the experience more pleasant, this putting green – complete with real grass – was built on top of an office building close to the River Thames.

How's this for a back swing, Dad? Miguel Angel Jiménez junior taking the chance to practice while his famous golf professional father is out competing in the 1997 Volvo Masters tournament at Montecastillo.

A fan gets into the swing of things during the 1998 US Open at the Olympic Club in California.

Golf giveth and golf taketh away – but it taketh away a hell of a lot more than it giveth.
Simon Hobday

Every golfer has a little monster in him – it's just that type of sport.
Fuzzy Zoeller

A big cheese in golf: one fan brings a bit of colour to the 1997 British Open at Royal Troon.

Follow the leader. British golf watchers cross a fairway during the 1996 British Open at Royal Lytham. With crowds increasing year by year, it is not unusual to see over 100,000 people attend major championships in Britain and the United States compared with just 2,000 back in the 1950s.

Golfers will stand for hours with their eyes glued on the ball, motionless, as does a cat watching the antics of its victim, then suddenly, as a spring released from tension, they burst into life and flog the ball in every possible direction except perhaps the right one.
H. MacNeile Dixon

The caddie shed at the 1989 US Masters at Augusta National where stories are swapped, confidences exchanged and the best card players in the world are to be found.

BEYOND REPROACH

Playing in a club competition at Los Angeles GC in 1950 Bob Gaared sliced his drive out of bounds on the 425-yard, par-4 2nd. The ball bounced off a tarmac road and into a passing truck. The driver heard the noise and stopped his vehicle next to the green. Having no idea of the rules of golf, he signalled that he had found the ball and placed it in the hole for safe-keeping. Gaared was convinced that he had made a one and entered it on his scorecard. Unfortunately his club committee disagreed and disqualified him for not having declared his first ball out-of-bounds and penalising himself two strokes. Surprisingly, even if Mr Gaared's mammoth effort had counted it would still not have been the 'longest' ace in history. That record goes to amateur Robert Mitera for his effort at the downhill 447-yard 10th hole at the appropriately named Miracle Hills GC in Omaha.

Previous page: Fred Astaire could literally turn his hand to anything. Asked to play a golf scene in a film, the legendary Hollywood star took an intensive series of lessons before he would pick up a club. As this photograph shows, his natural balance helped enormously and within days he could swing the club like a professional. In a later film he would perform a trick-shot routine where he danced around ten teed-up balls before striking them perfectly into the distance – one-handed!

◆ A classic encounter. This rare photograph of (left to right) Joyce Wethered, Roger Wethered, Robert T. Jones and Dale Bourne was taken shortly before the start of the 1930 British Amateur Championship at St Andrews. Partnering Bourne against the brother and sister combination, Bobby Jones would later describe Joyce Wethered as the best golfer he had ever played, saying: 'She did not miss one shot. She did not even half miss one half shot; and when we finished I could not help saying that I have never played golf with anyone, man or woman, amateur or professional, who made me feel so utterly outclassed.' By the end of the week Jones would win the British Amateur *en route* to taking his legendary Grand Slam of all four major championships. Four-time British Ladies champion Joyce Wethered dominated ladies golf in the 1920s. Known for her amazing concentration, she was playing an important match at Sheringham in Norfolk when a steam train went rattling by only yards from the green she was putting out on. Without a flicker she finished off and appeared surprised when someone asked whether the train had put her off. 'What train?' she replied.

Even Hitler and Hirohito couldn't stop America playing golf! This propaganda exercise shows top American golfers doing their bit for the US war effort in 1940.

PRIDE BEFORE A FALL?

George Duncan and Walter Hagen could not have been more opposite as personalities. Duncan was a tough, no-nonsense club professional from Manchester while the champagne-swilling American rarely travelled the world less than first class. Bitter rivals since the first Ryder Cup at Worcester, Massachusetts, in 1927, the two men rarely had a good word to say about each other. In 1929 that rivalry was put to the test once more at Moortown. They were chosen to captain their respective teams and Hagen drew first blood by leading his USA side to a 2½–1½ lead in the opening foursomes. Hagen was confident of victory and his reaction to drawing Duncan in the singles the following day was, 'Well boys, there's a point for our team right there.' Duncan was understandably furious. Refusing to shake hands on the first tee of their 36-hole match, the 1921 Open Champion came out with all guns blazing. He was spurred on by the large Yorkshire crowds and the atmosphere was intense as the partisan gallery cheered every putt the American missed. Rarely had Hagen been put under such pressure as when Duncan set an unofficial course record of 68 in the morning. Shortly after lunch the British player held a five-hole advantage. The match was effectively over and despite some long putts from the American at the end, Duncan had his revenge over the boastful Walter Hagen, eventually winning by the record margin of 10 and 8.

All smiles as Hollywood star Dorothy Lamour signs an autograph for British Ryder Cup professionals Charlie Ward and Dai Rees during a stop-off in New York in 1947. Sadly, it did not help team morale as a few days later in Portland the British lost eleven matches to one against the US.

WOMEN VS MEN

In 1910 an unusual 'battle-of-the-sexes' challenge match was arranged over Walton Heath and Sunningdale between the top female golfer, Cecil Leitch, and the top male golfer, Harold Hilton. Watched by thousands of interested onlookers, both players drove from the men's tees, but Leitch was compensated for her lack of strength by receiving a handicap allowance of one stroke every second hole. After four rounds in front of a large, mainly female, gallery, Leitch won by the narrow margin of 2 and 1. Not surprisingly, the match received a great deal of publicity, played as it was during a time when women's rights were at the forefront of the political agenda. It was hailed as a triumph for women everywhere. Hilton later refused a rematch.

AN UNUSUAL ADVANTAGE

Opera singer Orville Harold and lawyer John Walsh played an unusual match at the Wee Burn Country Club in Darien, Connecticut, in 1927. Wagering $200 on the result, the performer was allowed to sing out two high Cs during the match to compensate for his opponent's lower handicap. Unfortunately any hope he had of winning was lost because Walsh secretly wore earplugs throughout the entire match.

1951 British Open champion Max Faulkner was possibly the fittest winner in the event's long history. Employed by the Army to get marine commandos in shape during the Second World War, he returned to the professional game as assistant to Henry Cotton at Royal Mid-Surrey Golf Club. A true golfing maverick, he later showed a taste for colourful clothing and still remains the only player to have won the Open dressed in canary yellow plus fours!

Golf is like love. One day you think you're too old, and the next you can't wait to do it again.
Robert DeVincenzo

Group Captain Douglas Bader was a Second World War fighter ace despite losing both legs in a freak accident before 1940. Captured and sent to a prisoner-of-war camp in Germany, he tried to escape so many times that the camp commandant ordered the confiscation of his tin legs. Renowned for his huge determination, he never allowed his disability to get in the way of his daily round of golf.

Legendary comedian W.C. Fields receives a helping hand from a bevy of Hollywood beauties on his way to the golf course.

LEADERS	HOLE 1 PAR	
WADKINS B	1	
WADKINS L	1	3
EDWARDS		3
STRANGE		
NELSON		2
FUNK		0
WATSON		1
COLE		1
LUMAN		0
LANGER		2

Rising up the leader board. Model Danielle Cromb offers a pleasing alternative to the cut and thrust of competition during the 1987 United States PGA Championship at the PGA National Club, Florida.

The Bear versus the Shark. Jack Nicklaus, possibly the greatest golfer of all time, looks on as Greg Norman jokingly prostrates himself in front of him at the 1986 World Match Play Championship at Wentworth.

A Rolls-Royce golf buggy is the only way to travel, especially if you are Hollywood legend Victor Mature.

Monkey business. Long-time pals Bob Hope and Arnold Palmer take a break from filming *Call me Bwana* in 1960 to play around with a trained chimp.

A real hazard. Entrepreneur Billy Butlin decides to drop in during a golf exhibition given by Australian Bill Shankland in 1955. Butlin was never one to miss an opportunity for publicity, but the danger to all concerned is quite obvious.

A ROYAL AND ANCIENT GAME

🏐 Katherine of Aragon, first wife of Henry VIII, is known to have amused herself with golf while her husband was away pursuing other 'birdies'. In a letter to Cardinal Wolsey in 1513 she wrote, 'And all subjects be very glad, I thank God to be busy at the Golfe for my heart is very good to it.'

🏐 Sadly for Mary, Queen of Scots her passion for golf ultimately led to her downfall. At her trial she was accused of playing golf at Seton Fields near Musselburgh just days after the murder of her husband, Lord Darnley. Enough to discredit her in the eyes of her half-sister, Queen Elizabeth I, it was considered proof of her untrustworthy nature and was sufficient to send her to the axeman's block.

🏐 In 1457 King James II of Scotland outlawed golf because its growing popularity was interfering with compulsory archery practice for the common people, an important consideration with England threatening to invade from the south. He issued the now famous decree 'that Fute-baw and Golfe be utterly cryit done and nocht usit'. While it is not clear how much effect the ban actually had, it is certain that a public flogging would put a few modern-day golfers off their stroke.

🏐 King Charles I played golf most of his life. In 1642, before losing his head to Oliver Cromwell, he was found playing at Leith Links near Edinburgh when he received news of the Irish rebellion. He was thought to have continued his game with barely a shrug.

🏐 Away from royal life, Edward, Prince of Wales (later the Duke of Windsor) enjoyed the company of golfers. A reputedly shy man, he played and socialised with many of the top golfers of the day including Bobby Jones and Walter Hagen. He was never one to stand on ceremony and the story goes that after a game at a fashionable club in Surrey he invited English professional Archie Compston into the clubhouse for a drink. Apologising profusely, the club secretary then informed the royal visitor that professionals were not allowed inside and Compston would have to remain on the veranda. Spinning on his heels, Edward marched out of the door saying if it wasn't good enough for his guest, it would not be good enough for him. The club in question never did receive a 'royal' title like so many others.

◀ Back in the 1950s Gary Player pioneered the idea that golfers had to be as fit as any other professional sportsmen. Here he is at Royal Lytham in 1992 balancing two metal woods between his forefingers. If you think it looks easy, try it yourself.

➤ Taking Gary Player's advice to heart, a red-faced Lee Westwood uses the fitness unit that accompanies the players on tour in Europe.

HRH Prince Andrew escaping from the rough during the Alfred Dunhill Cup Pro-am at St Andrews in 1994. Following in the footsteps of other royal golfers like Mary, Queen of Scots, Charles I and Edward VIII, he has shown a real talent for the game in recent years.

Screen legend Clint Eastwood shows some determination as he cracks away a drive at the AT&T Pebble Beach Pro-am in 1995.

Bill Murray tees off with an exploding golf ball on the first tee of the 1998 AT&T Pebble Beach Pro-am watched by Clint Eastwood and top professional Rocco Mediate.

In the jungle, the mighty jungle, the wild thing sleeps tonight. A closely cropped John Daly appears a little uninterested at the 1995 United States PGA Championship at Riviera.

Listen to the News. Nick Faldo caddies for his rock-star pal Huey Lewis at the AT&T Pebble Beach Pro-am in California, 1997. Faldo nicknamed himself Fanny for the day; perhaps he thought no one would recognise him if he wore a wig.

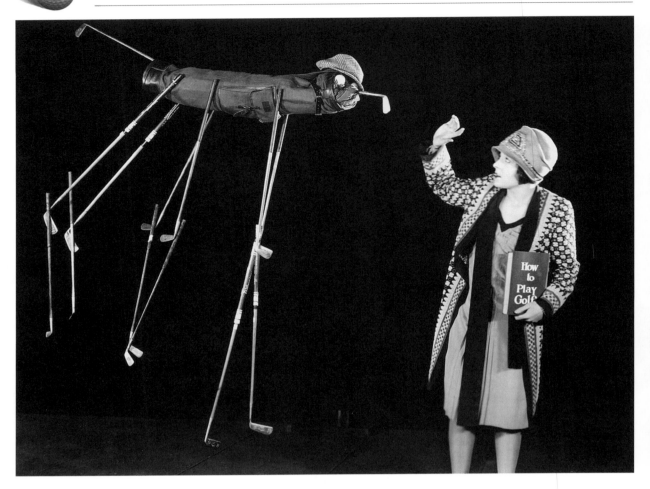

The Golf Bug: scientists working for the last twenty years have at last isolated the dreaded bug which affects anyone who takes up the sport – at least that was the story put out by one Hollywood film studio when promoting its latest starlet, Barbara Kent, in 1927.

LAST-MINUTE CALL UP

Bernard Darwin, golf correspondent of *The Times*, was in New York to cover the first Walker Cup match between Britain and the United States in 1922. On the last practice day team member Robert Harris fell ill and the hapless hack was invited to make up the numbers, which he did, losing both his matches. It was probably the first and last time any golf journalist had to write about his own shortcomings.

Previous page: Ferried back and forth to the golf course on the Santander ferry, ace prankster Mark Roe takes a tricky lie during the 1988 Spanish Open at Pedrena.

The frustrations of employing a caddie? This photograph reveals a very common 1920s stereotype: golfers were often well-to-do, military types wearing a monocle, while caddies were shifty, working-class characters who treated their employers with ill-disguised contempt.

Sand trapped at Valderrama in Spain. Ask yourself how he managed to walk to his shot without leaving a footprint.

◆ Taken at Coral Cables in Florida in 1939, this photograph shows Albert 'Sonny' Capone – the 20-year-old son of mobster Alfonse Capone. A talented golfer, he played to low single figures but never went anywhere without two armed bodyguards appointed by his father. And as the picture shows, they never strayed very far from his side on or off the golf course.

BEWARE OF THE WILDLIFE

Playing at Yaoundé in the Cameroon in 1985, a golfer was about to strike his ball when a snake wriggled between his legs. With barely a thought he altered the angle of his down swing and killed the reptile with a single blow. The question then arose whether this was deemed a stroke or not. He referred the matter to the ultimate authority – the Royal and Ancient Golf Club of St Andrews – and it was ruled that the action of 'transforming the snake from an outside agency to a loose impediment' was fully justified under the circumstances and as a result there would be no two-shot penalty.

At Muthaiga Golf Club in Kenya, home to the Tusker Kenya Open, there is a sign advising golfers not to run if any form of wildlife comes out of the bush – including leopards.

The holiday camp boom in the 1950s made mini-golf all the rage in Britain and this factory in Bolton designed and built many such courses.

In the early 1900s there was a strong fascination with anything African, as this photograph of Zulu warriors shows. It was printed as a postcard and the golf clubs were in reality walking sticks subtly altered for effect. A tennis ball substituted for a rather large golf ball.

In 1910 Buffalo Bill's Wild West Show rolled into London. Hoping to generate some publicity, a genuine Sioux chief and his daughter turned up at Sunningdale for a round of golf.

Can I have your autograph, Tiger? One fan adds to his pension fund by having a host of star names sign his cap during the 1997 US Open at Congressional.

◆ Getting a really good view. As many fans know, following the action at major golf tournaments can prove incredibly tough at times. Huge crowds hinder easy movement and just when you think you have a good view, a lumberjack-turned-steward stands right in front of you holding a sign that says 'Quiet please'. Not that this young woman had any problems getting a good position at Shinnecock Hills during the 1986 US Open.

Overleaf: Believe it or not, this was a serious 1920s pastime called Alpine golf. It was played along glaciers; the ball was painted black, then teed-up on the end of the player's skis before being struck off into the distance.

NOT ALWAYS THE BEST OF FRIENDS

Byron Nelson missed a golden opportunity to win the 1946 US Open at Canterbury Golf Club when his caddie accidentally kicked his ball off the 16th green during the third round. Incurring a one-stroke penalty, he missed out on the play-off by – you've guessed it – one stroke!

Raymond Russell had high hopes of a top-10 position going into the last round of the 2001 Compass English Open at the Forest of Arden course. However, these hopes were ruined at the 12th green when the Scottish professional threw his ball to the caddie for cleaning. Taking his eye off the ball, the caddie missed it then watched in horror as it rolled into a greenside lake. The caddie waded into the murky depths, but the result was a two-stroke penalty and almost £4,500 in prize money!

In the distant past St Andrews had a rule which stated that, 'If you should strike your caddie this will result in the loss of hole or one shot penalty.'

YOU'VE EITHER GOT IT . . .

Ryder Cup star Chick Harbert played an exhibition match against Walter Hagen during the Second World War and was desperate to beat the ageing legend. As they arrived on the final green both golfers were level and faced similar putts for birdie. Stepping up first, the youthful American got down on his stomach and lined up the putt as though his life depended on it. Confidently tapping the putt home he looked over at the nearly blind Hagen as if to say, 'Well, now it's your turn.' Hagen mimicked every movement his opponent had made to the letter, even going down on his stomach. Then he stepped up left handed and rolled the ball into the hole using the back of the putter head!

The biggest number ever posted in a professional tournament is 23 by Scottish-born Tommy Armour in the 1927 Shawnee Open. Even more remarkable is the fact that Armour had won the United States Open Championship the week before at Oakmont, defeating Harry 'Lighthorse' Cooper in a play-off.

Moe Norman was standing on the final tee in a pro tournament when he was informed by his caddy that all he needed to do to break the course record was to hit a driver, a 9 iron and take two putts. The legendary Canadian ball-striker then proceeded to hit a 9 iron off the tee, a driver off the fairway to the green, and take two putts to break the course record.

◀ I think it came from that direction, boss! A gob-smacked caddie reports back to professional Jim Payne during the European Masters in 1992 at Crans-sur-Sierre in Switzerland.

Australian trick-shot artist Joe Kirkwood actually performed this amazing shot for real. 'All I ask,' he said, 'is that my partner looks me squarely in the eye and I will do the rest. The only problem arises when she looks down at the ball and loses balance.'

☛ Owned by three-times British Open champion and club professional Henry Cotton, Pacifico the donkey caddie was among the most common sights at Penina in the 1970s. This young lady is showing her gratitude for a job well done.

◀ More monkey business. Baby Patsy and Joggs the chimp take a break from filming an Our Gang short entitled *Divot Diggers* in 1935. Quite who is most uncomfortable is uncertain.

The new sport of golf billiards or golf pool never took off in the United States, but here its inventor demonstrates how to play the game in the not-so-salubrious surroundings of an Arkansas lumber mill in 1915.

Golf is a game, which brings out the peculiarities and idiosyncrasies of human nature. It permits no compromises, recognises no weaknesses and punishes the foolhardy. Yet the apparent simplicity involved in hitting a small white ball from A to B lures all potential golfers into a false sense of security. Every instinct in the human psyche says the game looks easy, therefore it must be. That, for many of us, is where the trouble starts.
A.J. Dalconen

Because there was a shortage of land on which to practise live firing, Sandy Lodge Golf Club in Hertfordshire was taken over by the Army in 1914 as an artillery range. As you can see the flag is still in place on the first green as two young soldiers prepare to fire a machine gun towards the camera!

WARTIME RULES

 These rules were imposed by a golf club on England's south coast during the Second World War

❖ A ball moved, lost or destroyed by enemy action may be replaced without penalty as near as possible to where it originally lay.

❖ During gunfire or enemy action, players may take shelter without penalty for ceasing play.

❖ The positions of known delayed action bombs are marked by red and white flags and are placed at reasonably, but not guaranteed, safe distances.

❖ A ball lying in a bomb crater may be lifted and dropped without penalty.

❖ Players are asked to collect bomb and shell splinters from fairways to save damage to mowers. They may also be removed from the greens as loose impediments.

❖ If the ball enters a designated minefield, a new ball may be dropped without penalty within two-club lengths, not nearer the hole.

With the threat that German paratroopers might land at any moment, in 1940 golfers on the south coast of England were strongly advised to carry a rifle in their golf bags. If there was not enough room, then perhaps the caddie should have one readily available.

➤ During the Second World War many golf courses were closed for the duration but that did not stop local kids in Scarborough from making their own course among the bombed-out ruins of a row of houses. Using the former gardens as a green, they were in danger of being arrested but, as always, boys will be boys.

In the 1920s, long before the Egyptian authorities banned tourists from climbing the Great Pyramids, hitting a golf ball from one to the other was a popular pastime, even if the golfer pictured was risking life and limb by wearing fashionably heeled shoes. What non-golfing tourists felt about having a ball land on their head from such a great height is not recorded.

One theory – a Freudian one for what it is worth – is that man, in striding around hitting a golf ball, is satisfying some deep primeval jungle instinct. Instead of chasing through the forest with not much on but a piece of cloth in the right place, and hunting animals with bow and arrow, he puts on plus-fours and beats a golf ball all over the countryside in order to satisfy some complex, unfathomable desire.
'Onlooker'

Hoping to highlight the curse of slow play, Major John Bywaters, former secretary of the British Professional Golfers' Association, set up this rather unusual picture in 1976. He insisted that a round of golf should not take more than three hours for an amateur fourball: the average today has crept past the four-hour mark.

We are told that the great golfer is born and not made; and it is held by the best authorities that success in golf is very largely due to the possession of exactly the right temperament for the game. Generally speaking, that is a cold, phlegmatic sort of temperament, one that permits of its possessor remaining unmoved and steadily persevering towards his object in spite of a multitude of disturbing elements by which he may be surrounded, and notwithstanding the most outrageous ill-fortune with which he may be afflicted.
Henry Leach

Look closely and you will see the golfer who is putting is blindfolded. Another odd challenge match from Sunningdale in the 1920s, the only 'advantage' offered to the non-sighted player was having his caddie shout instructions as to where the hole was and how much slope to allow for!

Birdies and babes. Known for his crazy sense of fun, European Tour professional Mark Roe decides to play from the ladies' tee prior to the 1989 English Open at Royal Birkdale. Not only that, he also decides to don a dress for the occasion.

A jumbo-sized golfer. Rosie the elephant became a minor celebrity in the Miami area of Florida when it was found she could hit drives well over 240 yards by swinging a golf club with her trunk! Trained by owner John Brophy (in the black sweater), she is shown out-hitting local professional Willie Klein in 1930.

The most exquisitely satisfying act in the world of golf is that of throwing a club. The full back swing, the delayed wrist action, the flowing follow-through, followed by that unique whirring sound, reminiscent only of a passing flock of starlings, are without parallel in sport.
Henry Longhurst

THE ROUND OF HIS LIFE

According to the record books, the oldest golfer ever to make a score to equal his age was Arthur Thompson of British Columbia. At the age of 103 he scored 103 on the testing Uplands Golf Club in Victoria.

Is this the longest hole in the world? Taking one year and 114 days, amateur golf nut Floyd Rood played his way across the United States. Travelling approximately 3,400 miles, he hit 114,737 shots (including 3,511 penalty shots) and wore out a dozen pairs of golf shoes on the way.

One player who would never be penalised for slow play is American amateur Dick Kimbrough. In 1972 he set a new speed record by completing eighteen holes at the 6,068-yard North Platte Country Club in Nebraska in exactly 30 minutes and 10 seconds. Carrying just a three-iron he ran between shots and still broke 100 for the round.

In 1976 airline pilot Alain Reisco set the record for playing golf on three different continents in one day. Starting at the Royal Mohammedia Golf Club in Morocco, he then played at Torrequebrada near Malaga in Spain in the afternoon before ending the day in New York at the North Hills Country Club.

NEVER GIVE UP

Determined to finish out the hole during the 1913 Shawnee Invitational Tournament at Shawnee-on-Delaware, Pennsylvania, Mrs J. Meehan hit her tee-shot into the fast running Binniekill River which fronted the 16th green. Rather than take a penalty drop, the plucky lady clambered into a nearby row boat and set off after her still floating ball. Taking every opportunity to take a swipe she eventually made dry land after 40 attempts. Undeterred by the fact she was now a mile or more downstream, she hacked her way through dense undergrowth until she finally reached the green. Two weary putts later she holed out for a card-wrecking score of 161.

TOO FAST, TOO SLOW?

Mark Calcavecchia and John Daly were both fined by the PGA Tour for playing too quickly. Out first, they completed the final round in the 1999 Tournament Players' Championship at Sawgrass in 2 hours and 3 minutes. Daly fired an 80 and Calcavecchia an 81.

Making a 72-hole tournament look like a mere sprint, the longest event ever was the World Open at Pinehurst in 1973. Played over two weeks and 144 holes, the halfway cut must have come as a relief to many.

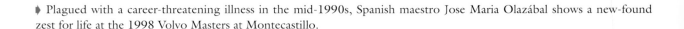

♦ Plagued with a career-threatening illness in the mid-1990s, Spanish maestro Jose Maria Olazábal shows a new-found zest for life at the 1998 Volvo Masters at Montecastillo.

THE LAST WORD

Golf is a game in which perfection stays just out of reach.
Betsy Rawls

Golf does strange things to other people too. It makes liars out of honest men, cheats out of altruists, cowards out of brave men, and fools out of everybody.
Milton Gross

Golf is the Esperanto of sport. All over the world golfers talk the same language – much of it nonsense and much unprintable – endure the same frustrations, discover the same infallible secrets of putting, share the same illusory joys.
Henry Longhurst

No matter what happens never give up a hole. . . . In tossing in your cards after a bad beginning you also undermine your whole game, because to quit between tee and green is more habit-forming than drinking a highball before breakfast.
Sam Snead